LET'S GO ON .....
PICNIC

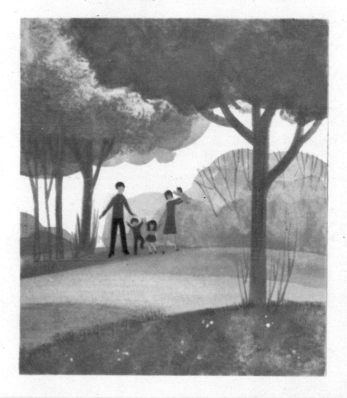

 A MOTHER-AND-CHILD PLAYBOOK PREPARED BY YOUNG WORLD PRODUCTIONS LTD. IN CONSULTATION WITH THE PRE-SCHOOL PLAYGROUPS ASSOCIATION

© 1972 Young World Productions Ltd.

SBN 72380888 0

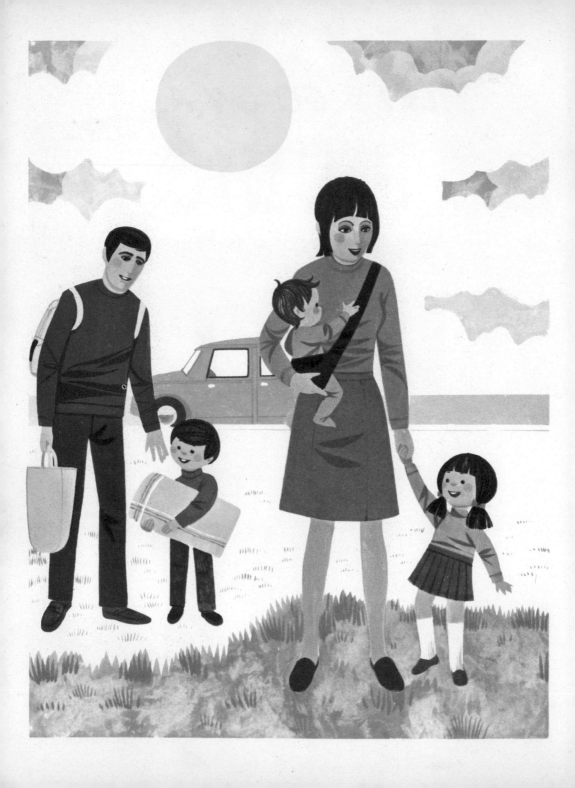

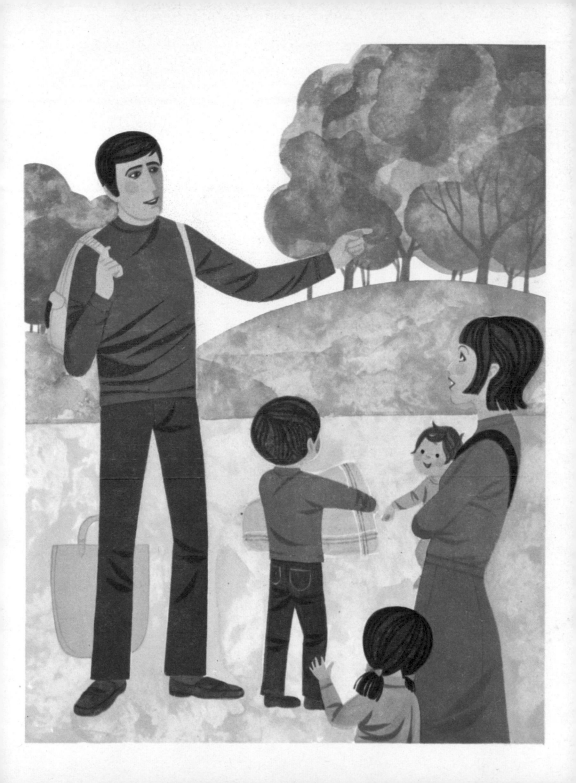

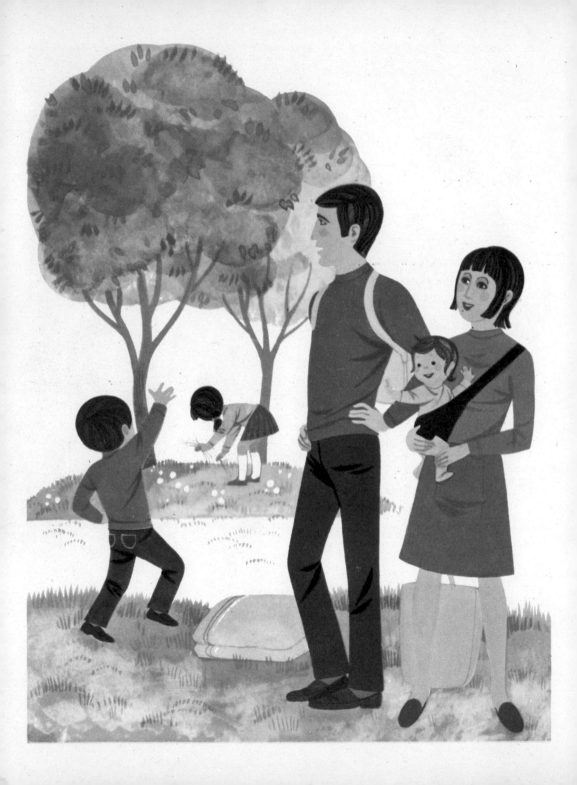

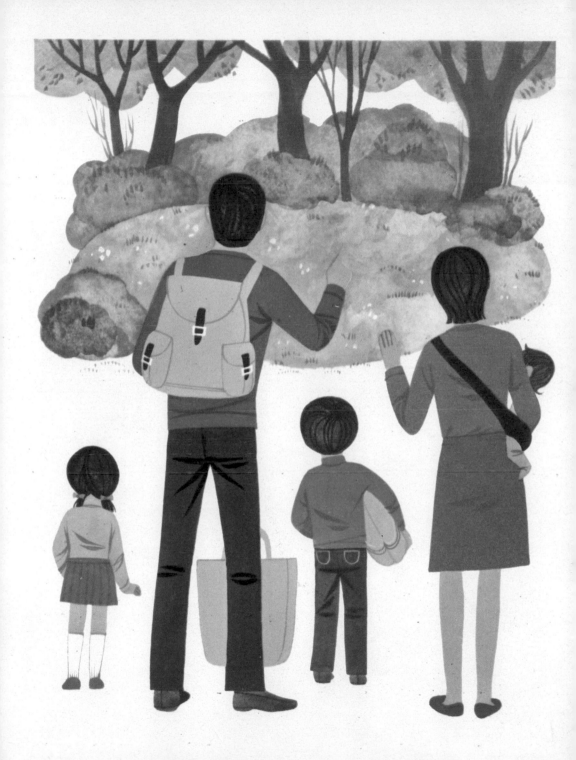

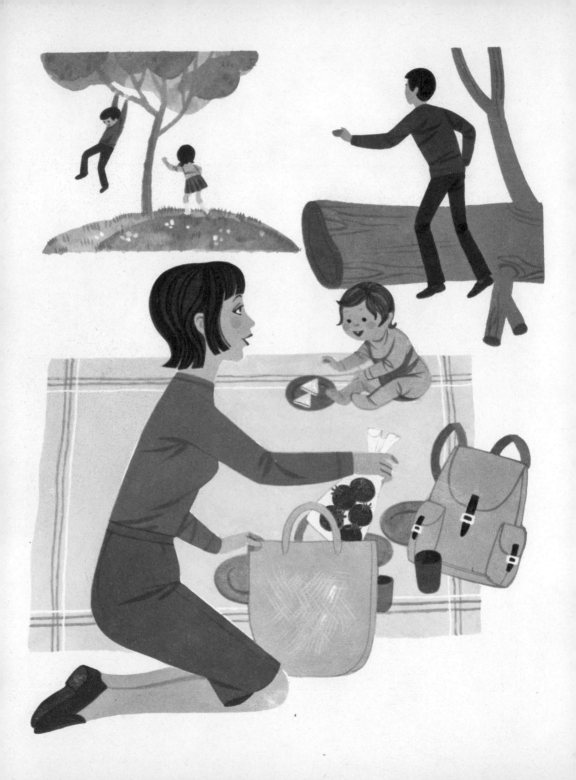

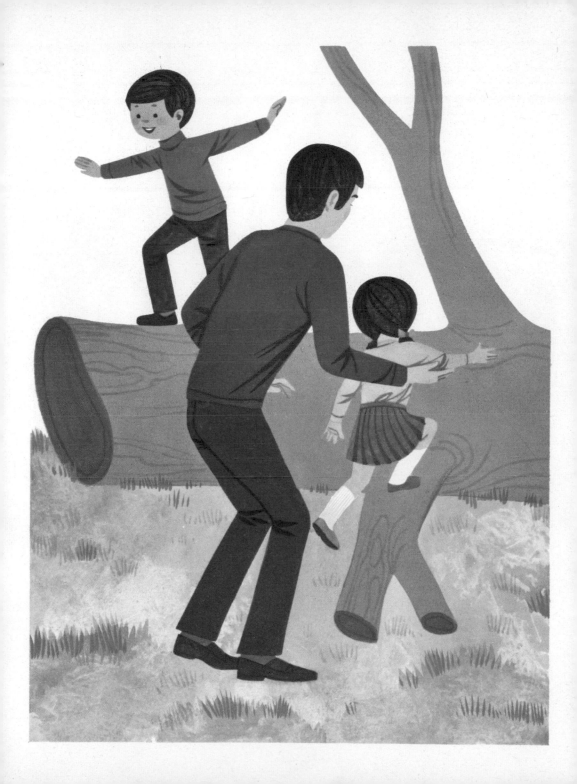

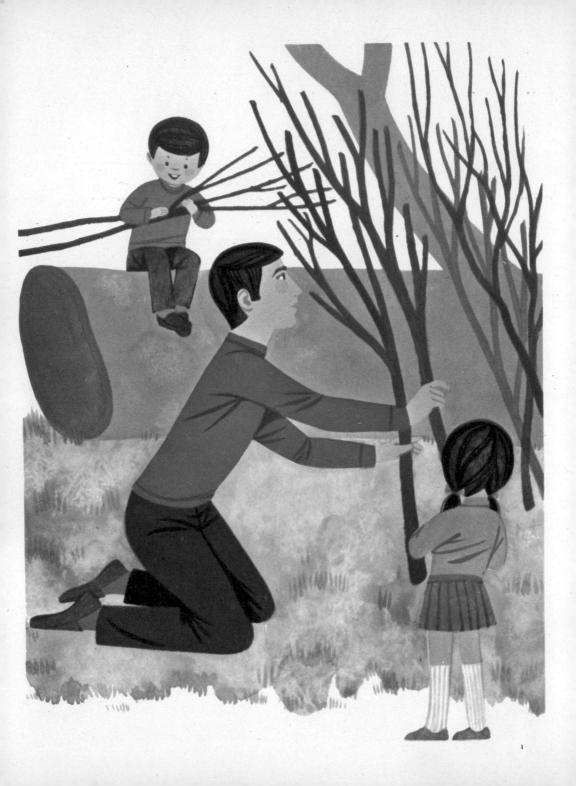

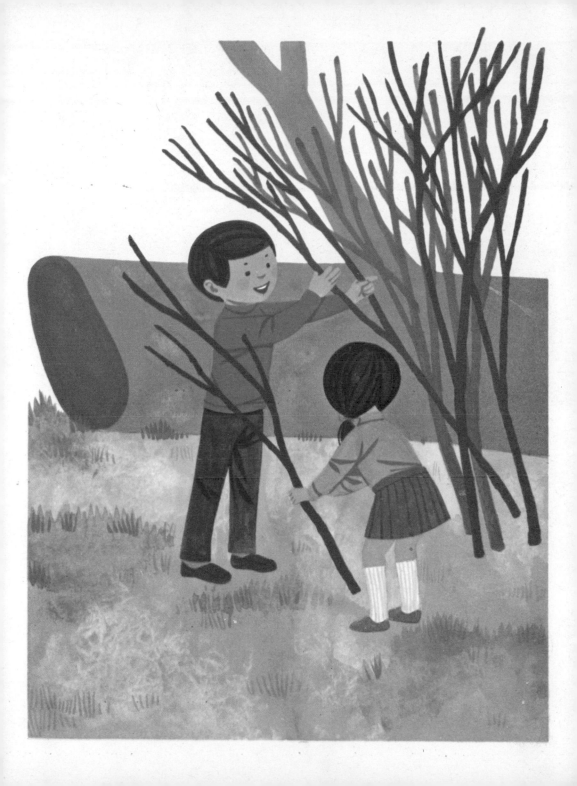

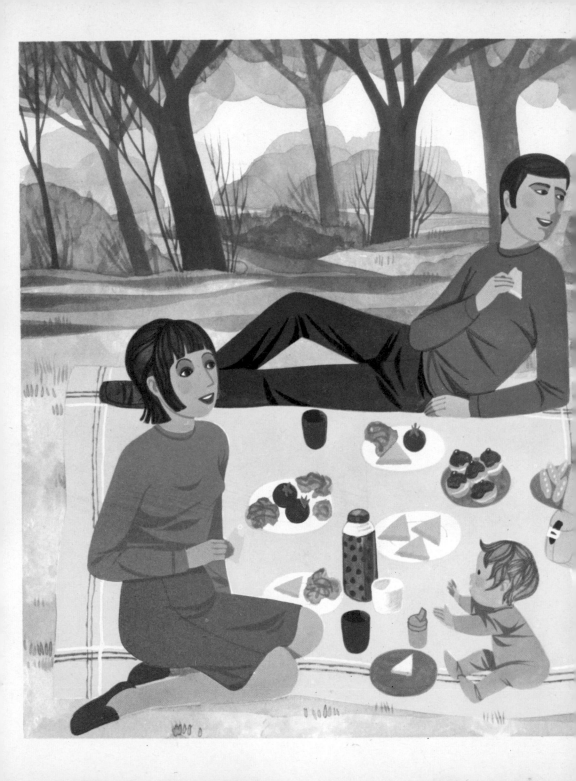

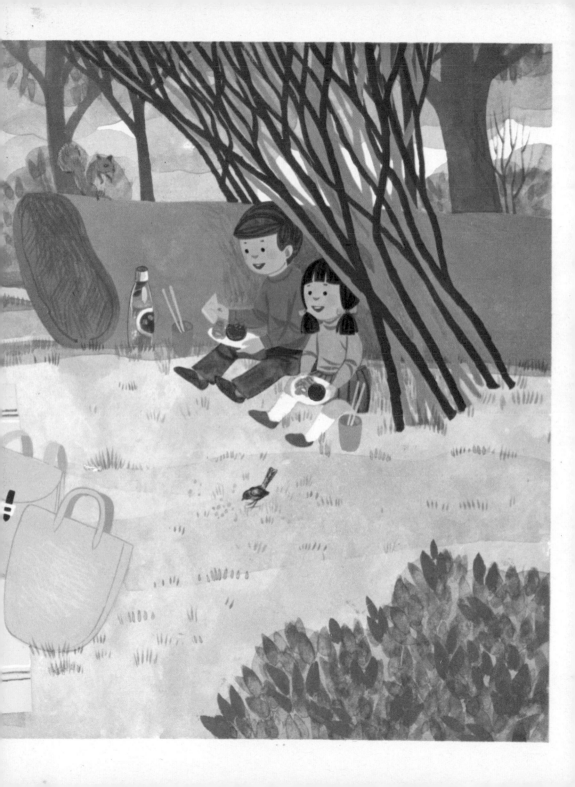

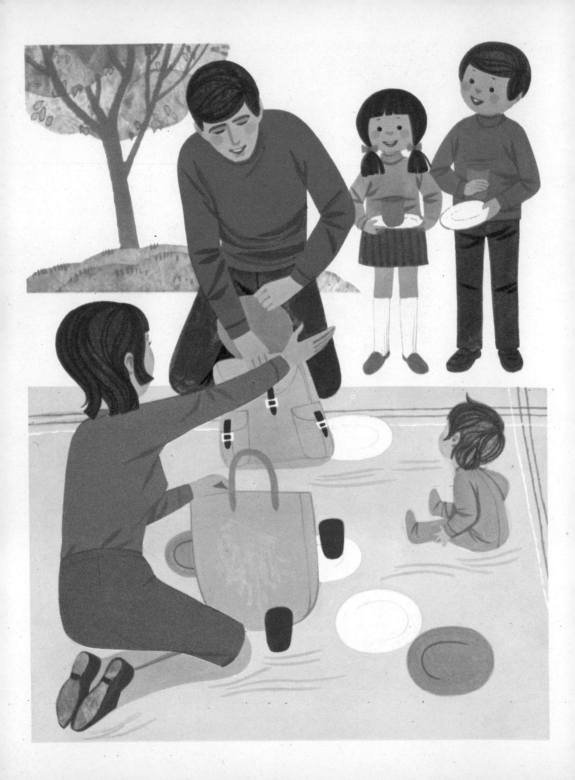

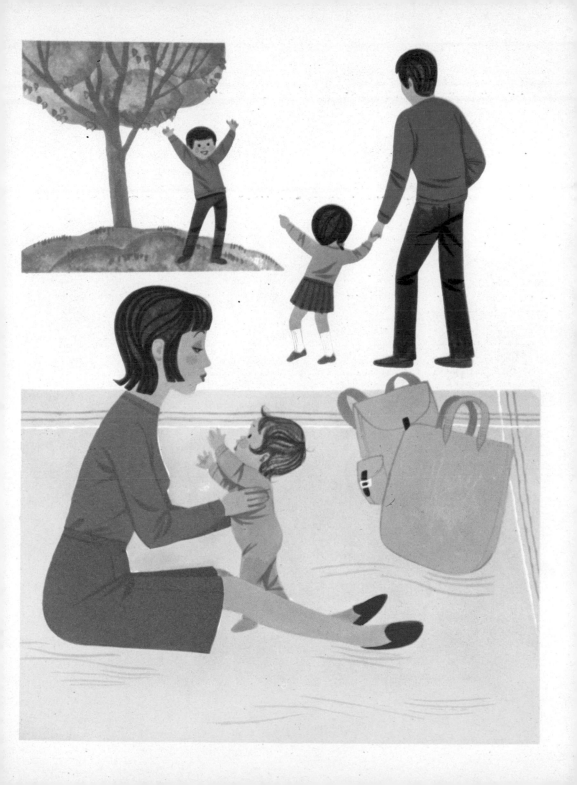

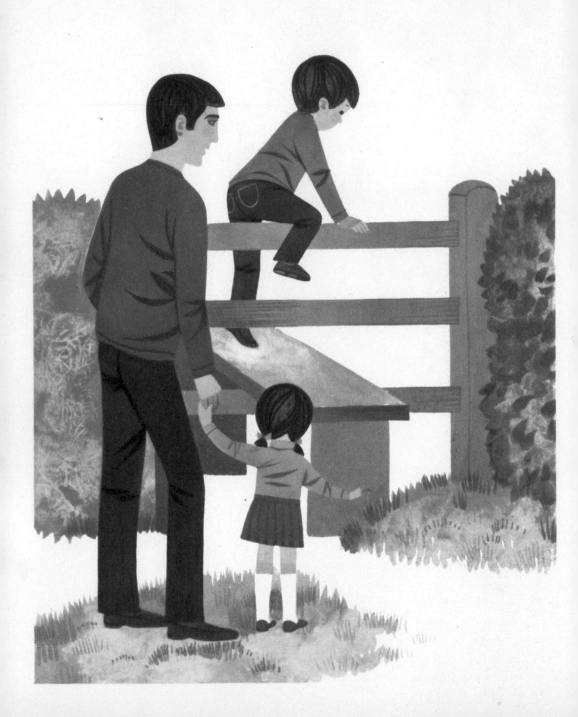

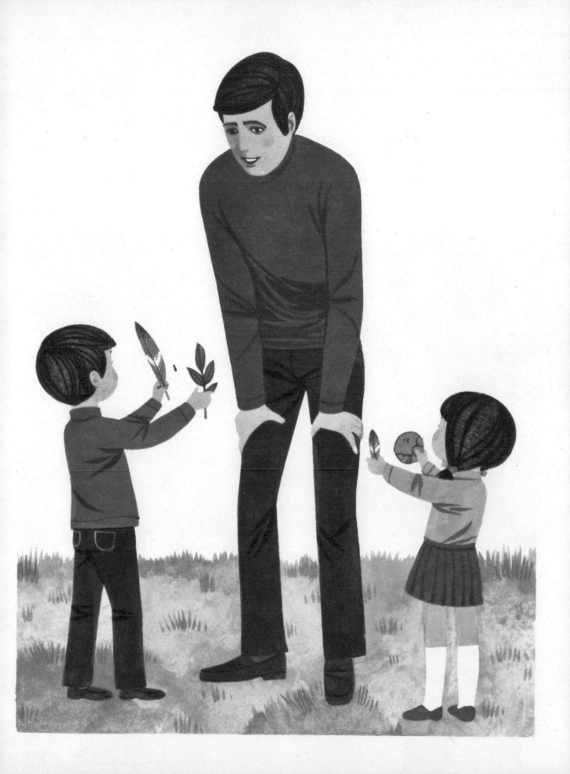

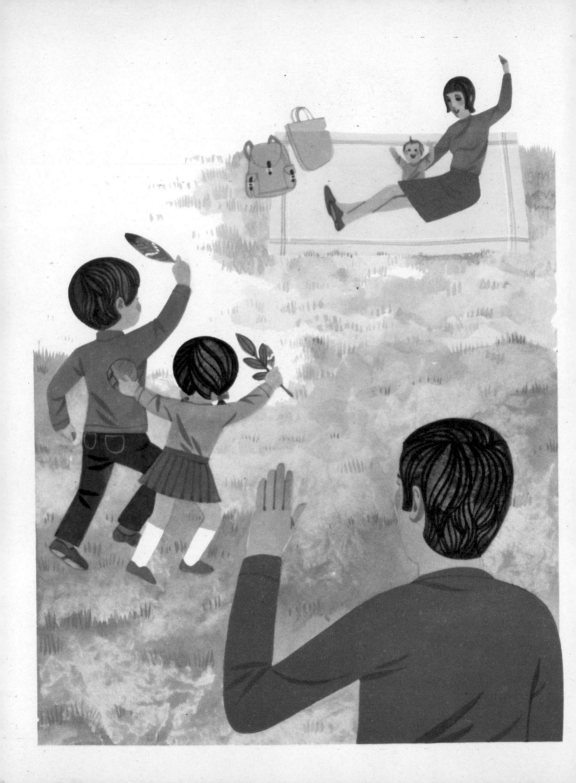

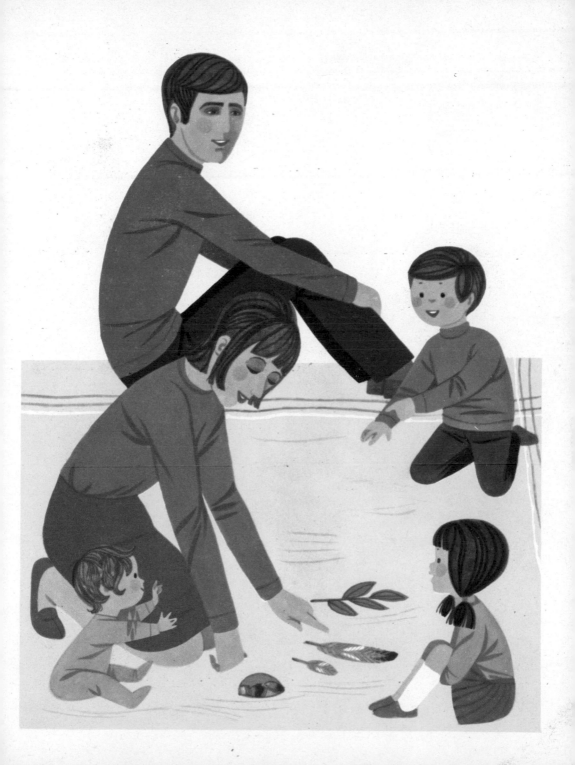

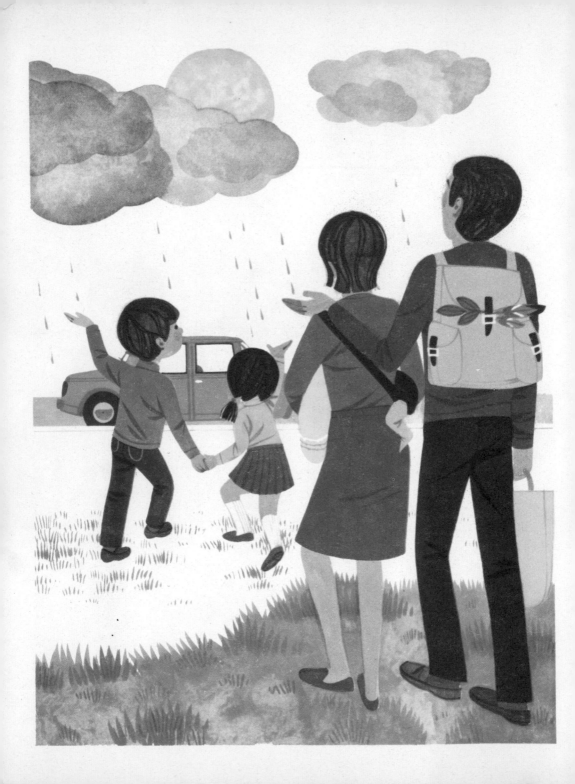

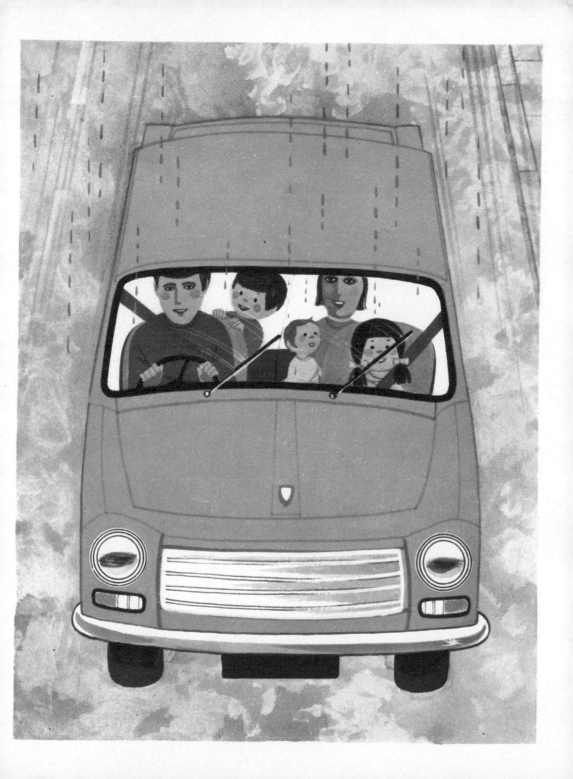

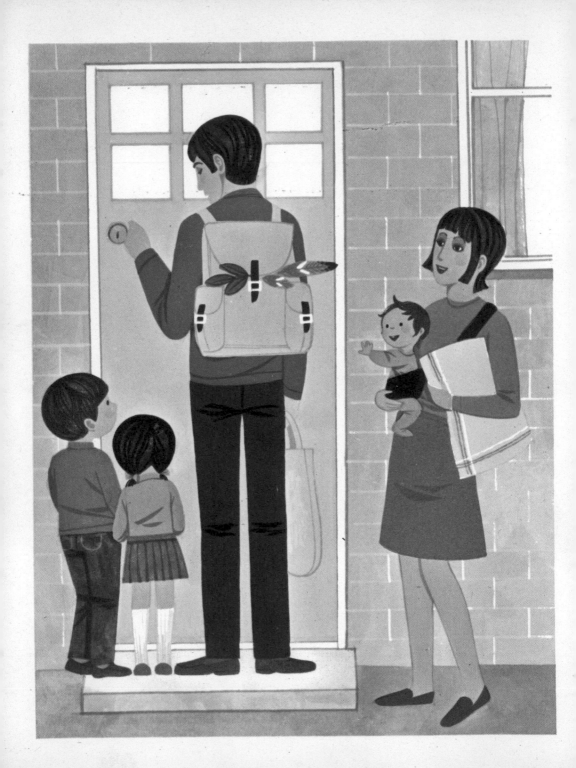